THE HEALTHY PROFESSIONAL WRITER

BUSINESS FOR BREAKFAST, VOLUME 6

LEAH R CUTTER

KNOTTED ROAD PRESS

The Healthy Professional Writer
Business for Breakfast, Volume 6
Copyright © 2017 Leah Cutter
All rights reserved
Published by Knotted Road Press
www.KnottedRoadPress.com

ISBN: 978-1-943663-63-7

Cover and interior design copyright © 2017 Knotted Road Press
http://www.KnottedRoadPress.com

Never miss a release!
If you'd like to be notified of new releases, sign up for my newsletter.

I only send out newsletters once a quarter, will never spam you, or use your email for nefarious purposes. You can also unsubscribe at any time.

http://www.LeahCutter.com/newsletter/

All rights reserved. Except for brief quotations in critical articles or reviews, the purchaser or reader may not modify, copy, distribute, transmit, display perform, reproduce, publish, license, create derivative works from, transfer or sell any information contained in this book without the express written permission of Leah Cutter or Knotted Road Press. Requests to use or quote this material for any purpose should be addressed to Knotted Road Press.

Disclaimer
This book is provided for general educational purposes. While the author has used her best efforts in preparing this book, Knotted Road Press makes no representation with respect to the accuracy or completeness of the contents, or about the suitability of the information contained herein for any purpose. All content is provided "as is" without warranty of any kind.

ALSO BY LEAH R CUTTER

The Shadow Wars Trilogy

The Raven and the Dancing Tiger

The Guardian Hound

War Among the Crocodiles

The Clockwork Fairy Kingdom

The Clockwork Fairy Kingdom

The Maker, the Teacher, and the Monster

The Dwarven Wars

Seattle Trolls

The Changeling Troll

The Princess Troll

The Fairy-Bridge Troll

Contemporary Fantasy

Siren's Call

The Immortals' War

The Cassie Stories

Poisoned Pearls

Tainted Waters

Spoiled Harvest

The Chronicles of Franklin

The Popcorn Thief
The Soul Thief

INTRODUCTION

This isn't a standard Business for Breakfast book. This book is as much about my personal journey to health as anything else.

I've always considered myself healthy. However, when I start detailing out what I've been through, it surprised me how sick I actually have been. I started getting sick on a regular basis about the time I was twenty eight. I didn't realize until my mid-forties that I actually had an undiagnosed thyroid condition.

In addition, I've had migraines my entire life—nothing horrible, but they occurred every month, without fail, sometimes only a couple, sometimes more. Then, starting in 2015, my migraines suddenly became chronic. I ended up with twelve to fifteen migraines a month, with headaches almost every day. I basically lost half my time.

I still wrote.

In spring of 2017, I changed my diet dramatically, and I found a way of dealing with my migraines. Now, in September of 2017, I can tell you that I'm down to one migraine per month, with only one severe headache as well. (I'm hoping over the next few months, as my brain heals, that I can stop having migraines all together.)

I started regularly blogging about my diet and my health. I tried to post once a week about where I was at, what was happening. It was a form of accountability, as it were. It helped me stick to the diet and

INTRODUCTION

the new migraine treatments, even when I had migraines lasting for forty-eight hours or more.

Other people have found my journey inspirational. I've have more than one person tell me that they wanted me to write a book about it so that they could buy it and give it to their friend/brother/spouse, what have you.

This book is set up with alternate chapters: one chapter is more focused on health, while the next is more focused on being a healthier writer and "leveling up" your writing.

I hope this book helps you with your process and your own personal journey.

Please, feel free to contact me or leave me a message on Facebook if you want to go into more depth about the things you're experiencing.

Take care, happy (and healthy!) writing –

Leah Cutter
September 2017

CHAPTER ONE

I started getting migraines when I was 18, back in 1980, i.e., the dark ages. No one in my family suffered from migraines, so I had no idea what was happening to me. This was a long time before the internet, so it wasn't as if I could go look up my symptoms.

Plus, pain wasn't my primary issue. While my head hurt, I also had a bunch of other things going on. For example, the migraines affected my inner ear. I started losing my balance and walking into things. My roommates accused me of being drunk when I wasn't.

More scary than that, I developed tunnel vision during a migraine. The edges of my sight grew dark. I was afraid I was going blind.

Fortunately, the hospital I went to correctly diagnosed my migraines. The doctor prescribed Maxalt, which I considered my miracle drug for decades.

Eventually, I figured out my primary triggers: stress, and my period. Which meant I was pretty much guaranteed at least two migraines every month, generally before my cycle started, and sometime during my cycle.

But the pills worked. After I took one, the pain would go away after about twenty minutes. I would, however, end up having three to four hours of feeling brainless. If it had been a bad migraine, I'd have an additional another six to twelve hours of feeling fragile, but being able to work. I considered it a good bargain: not able to function well for a few hours versus a few days.

Fast forward to 2006. I was pretty sick, and had been for years. Fortunately, I'd found a wonderful naturopath who treated my symptoms, not the numbers on my blood test.

He diagnosed my thyroid condition: I was hypothyroid, that is, my body didn't produce enough of the thyroid hormones on its own.

While I'd had other turning points in my life, this was one of the biggest ones.

What is Healthy?

I'd taken medicine off and on all my life. But the pattern was: get sick, take medicine, get well.

This was the first time I'd had to change my personal definition of what was being well. I was going to have to take medication every day for the rest of my life.

Did that mean I was sick?

Side Note

This is the first side note. They will be scattered through out the book.

I urge you: you might skip or skim the rest of the text, but please read all the side notes. There will be assignments here, meditations and questions you need to think about.

Meditation: what does it mean, to you, to be sick? What does being well mean to you?

Spend time with these questions. They are essential to your ultimate health.

There is no right or wrong answer. But how will you know if you're well if you haven't defined what that is for yourself?

Meds

I sat with the above questions, defining my healthiness and sickness, for a long time.

I finally came up with the following:

Beyond the continuum from sick to well, there's another axis: healthy.

I had a chemical imbalance, and though it had only recently been diagnosed, I'd probably had it since I was 28. (I was in my mid-40s when I was diagnosed.)

In order to be healthy, I had to take medication. It didn't mean I was weak, or sick, or that I had to feel ashamed. It just meant I had this pill to take every morning.

It also didn't mean I was old, though I guess I kind of am, being in my fifties now.

Side Note

I read a study about this same time that had found that people's tastes froze at a frighteningly young age. By mid to late twenties, people's tastes in music, clothes, food, had all set, and they'd stopped trying new things.

I decided at that time to start what I call, "the anti-stodgy campaign."

Every month, I make sure to try something new. A new restaurant, a new route home, a new recipe, a new way of doing things.

It has led to some wonderful discoveries, as well as some awesome failures.

Meditation: when was the last time you tried something utterly new? How does the thought of trying new things make you feel?

If you don't feel excited, nervous or scared, but just blah, I suggest that you aren't actually reaching for something new, that you are dreaming too small. (Unless you've already implemented your own anti-stodgy campaign, in which case, carry on.)

One of the things that at the very least keeps me young at heart is the fact that I try new things on a regular basis. This, for me, is part of being healthy.

How can you implement your own anti-stodgy campaign? Should you put a monthly reminder in your calendar to ask, "Have you tried something new this month?" Would putting it in a quarterly reminder work better? Should it become one of your random screen savers that you'll see every once in a while as the pictures cycle through?

Your health may not be at a point where you can try something new regularly: it might be too exhausting for you currently. I still want you to think about it. Trying new things on a regular basis should become part of your definition of healthy.

Diabetes Scare

Sometime in 2006-2007, as part of a regular check up, my naturopath tested my A1C. This test measures the amount of sugar that your red blood cells have been exposed to over the last three months. (NOTE: I am aware that the A1C is horribly flawed.)

The results showed that I was in the pre-diabetic stage. There was far, far too much sugar in my blood.

A glucose tolerance test showed again, a lot of sensitivity to sugar.

Well, shit.

I went on what I then called my *horribly restrictive diet*. There were so many things that I couldn't eat and I was desperately unhappy about it.

I bet you can guess how successful I was with this diet, given what I'd originally named it.

That turned out to not be the case. I couldn't maintain the diet, but it was successful in very unexpected ways.

The diet involved not eating gluten or any sugar. Low carb all the way. Low fat, too. Given how often I ate out (three-four times per week) it was kind of a pain in the ass.

However.

Something I hadn't really noticed was that I had constant headaches. They were so regular and happened almost every day that I didn't think anything of them.

It wasn't until I went on the *horribly restrictive diet* that I realized how many headaches I had.

For the first time in years, I suddenly didn't have a headache. Hmmmm.

After a few weeks, I was at a party and I had a small piece of birthday cake. Within about thirty minutes, I had a headache.

I drew the obvious conclusion: Sugar was bad for me. I'd never been addicted to sugar, I preferred savory to sweet.

I couldn't stick to the *horribly restrictive diet*. It was almost a paleo diet, but I was still eating grains (healthy grains!) as well as no fat.

I was hungry all the time and unhappy as well. Even though the diet helped my health, and greatly reduced the number of headaches I had, the side effects were too great and in the end, it just wasn't worth it.

However, as my blood work was now normal, I never went back to eating a lot of sugar. I still ate more than my body could handle on a regular basis, and just dealt with the headaches.

Side Note

Question: What are you doing right now that you know is unhealthy for you, but you do it anyway?

WHY do you do it anyway?

Be honest.

Is it just an occasional indulgence? Or is there some level of self-punishment involved?

Do you deserve to be healthy?

Is your self-identity tied up in your sickness?

I'll come back to these questions later. But you might want to start thinking about these things now.

CHAPTER TWO

Of course, during all of that, I was still writing. Not as diligently as I do now, and certainly not as quickly. But I still wrote through all the ups and down and being healthy as well as times of actually being sick.

I was sick quite often. Every four to six weeks I came down with that I called an *exhaustion cold*. I had mild cold symptoms and complete exhaustion. I'd sleep for two to three days, then I'd get up and go again.

I was never certain if I had the worst immune system in the world and I was always coming down with whatever was going around, or if I had the best immune system and I only caught mild versions of what was going around.

Turned out, it was neither.

Not having enough thyroid hormones in your system makes you tired. Because I am a touch stubborn, (just a touch, mind you) I never slowed down or stopped. I just kept going, and literally drove myself into exhaustion every four to six weeks. I did this for decades.

Back to the writing, which I still did a lot of, even when I was completely exhausted.

At that time, I was writing out my first draft long hand. Then I'd type it up. By the time the typed draft was finished, the manuscript was somewhat clean, but still broken.

Writing long hand takes muscles. You need to strengthen your hands, as well as take care of your wrists, or else you'll cripple yourself.

Typing takes muscles too. And again, care to make sure you don't damage yourself.

Writing is a physical activity. You need to prepare for it in order to stay healthy.

Breaks

I know, I know. Everyone talks about the importance of taking breaks. I can hear the cries already: "But if I stop, I'll break the flow of words!"

My response? If stopping breaks your flow, then you weren't really in flow state in the first place.

I'll talk more about training for flow state later. It's part of the physical training that you need to engage in to survive writing.

This is just the start of your physical training for writing.

Think about running. You don't start off running 5K the first time you get off your couch.

You walk around the block.

Then you walk around two blocks.

Then maybe, a few days later, you walk half a mile. Then a mile. Finally, you start jogging. You walk and run. Like that.

Writing is the same way. You must train for it. Start off with one hundred, two hundred, five hundred words.

However. More words while being unhealthy is self-defeating in the long run. You'll damage your wrists, your arms, even your hands if you don't train for it first.

And part of that training is teaching yourself how to stop and start the flow so you can take breaks.

Breaks are essential to your long term health.

You will need to find the mechanism that works for you in terms of taking a break, as well as the amount of time between breaks.

Me? I use timers on my computer. (Dejal/timeout for the Mac, Workrave.org for the PC.) I respect those timers.

Every twenty minutes, I must stretch for thirty seconds. Every fifty-five minutes, I must get up and walk away from the computer for five minutes. Generally during that time, I try to get in one thousand steps by walking around the block. (Or I change the laundry around. Or do the dishes. Something physical that's away from the computer.)

Then I sit back down and I start writing again.

Writers are stubborn creatures. Contrary. Ornery. Many won't respect the timer on their computer. So they have to find something else.

I know one writer who sets a kitchen timer across the room. When it goes off, she *must* stop her writing to go shut the dang thing off.

I know another writer who sets a timer on her phone, but then puts the phone in another room to help him get out of his writing room.

There are some writers who claim that they drink enough tea/water/beverage-of-choice that their bladder forces them to get up and use the restroom once an hour.

I have spent time with these writers, while they were writing. No matter what their claim, they did not get up and take enough breaks, certainly not once an hour, more like once every three to four hours.

Maybe you'll be different. Time it. Chances are, you won't be, and you'll need to come up with some other system.

But you must figure out a way to take breaks. Or you'll damage your body, and not be able to write. And that would be tragic.

Dictation

I know some writers who have great success dictating their work. The software for taking dictation has certainly gotten a lot better than it used to be. If you're having problems with hands and need to find a better solution than typing, you may want to look into dictation.

It takes time to train yourself to speak your work out loud. One writer said it took her about three weeks. Another writer told me it took him about three months. It isn't a process that you can merely switch to just to try. You have to commit to it for a while before you can figure out if it will be right for you.

Some of the writers I know who do dictation have found that they are able to produce many more words per hour, even after they edit what they dictated. Other writers have found very little increase in their productivity, because they still end up doing so much editing later. Your milage may vary.

Side Note

Question: What is your process for writing? Long hand? Computer outline then draft then rewrite? Dictation followed by edits?

How does the thought of trying a different form make you feel?

The answer to that second question will tell me about your path as a writer.

Most beginning writers, that is, those with less than ten novels under their belts, will not feel comfortable changing their process. They've found what works for them, thank you very much.

Most mid-term writers, that is, those with less than twenty novels under their belts, will be rather blasé about the idea of changing their process. They might try something new someday. They might not.

Long term writers, with more than twenty novels under their belts, know that the process changes, whether you want it to or not.

For me, my writing process today bears little resemblance to even what I was doing a year ago. I suspect that in a year's time, it will be different again.

Productivity

If you've read the first Business for Breakfast book, you'll note that I call the software I use to schedule my breaks my "productivity software".

I know, it's counterintuitive. You're taking breaks! How can you be more productive?

Because I am taking breaks, I can work more hours. Instead of focused writing for two to three hours with no breaks, I can do four or five hours, with breaks. I get a lot more done.

And remember, this is from the woman who drove herself into complete utter exhaustion on a regular basis.

Train yourself to take breaks. It isn't any more natural to take breaks than it is to type or dictate words. (Telling stories is completely natural.) You had to learn how to type. You dedicated the time to learn how to dictate.

Now, train yourself to take breaks. Your body will thank you for it.

CHAPTER THREE

When I was a kid, I had allergy tests done. Turned out I was allergic to all kinds of grasses and most trees and well, pretty much everything green.

I used to joke that I had seasonal allergies—just that I was allergic to every season. I lived on antihistamines, would panic if I ran out of tissue, and generally had three to four sinus infections every year, frequently timed to the changing of the seasons.

In 2009, I came down with atypical walking pneumonia. To add insult to injury, I had a sinus infection on top of it.

I was so sick. I creaked when I sat up. Freaked my kitty out—she knew that sound was unhealthy.

I was sick and tired of being sick and tired all the time. I'd fixed my thyroid hormones by then. Why was I still getting so many sinus infections? What could I do about it?

I went looking for answers out on the internet, as one does when one is fevered and not completely straight in the head.

The wisdom of the internet told me that I should cut out all grain. Not just go gluten free, but cut out all wheat, rice, corn, oats, etc. In addition, I should cut out all sugar and all mushrooms.

I was desperate at that point. I'd tried gluten free before and hadn't really seen any change in my health. I was already not eating a lot of sugar.

Why not try this?

Within a week, I was feeling better than I had in a long, long while.

Within two weeks, I knew I was *never* going back to my old way of eating.

My sinuses cleared up. I stopped taking antihistamines. Since I started eating this way (back in 2009) I've had two sinus infections. That's it.

I didn't lose weight, because I wasn't overweight to begin with. I did lose inches all around. I lost half a ring size. Because I was wearing my Vibram Five Finger shoes at the time, I was able to tell that my toes shrank in diameter.

When I was eating grain, I was constantly inflamed and swollen. I was allergic to all the things I was putting in my mouth. AND I NEVER REALIZED IT!

Finding the right diet, that is, the diet that works best FOR ME, made all the difference.

Side Note

Do you know what type of diet works best for you and your body? Or are you still working to figure that out?

The diet I currently follow would literally kill some of my friends. Their bodies cannot process the foods that I eat regularly. Conversely, eating a vegetarian diet would kill me. I eat more vegetables than most vegetarians already, but I still need meat and meat protein.

Remember that anti-stodgy campaign I talked about earlier? Part of being healthy means determining the diet that actually helps you be healthy. Not the diet that fits your ideology, or your personal causes, or even your partner's diet.

This can be a huge step for some people. Food is very personal. I'll talk more about that later.

But for now, I want you to think about what foods you're feeding your body. What makes your body feel good?

NOTE: I am NOT talking about the foods that your mouth finds tasty, but that give you an upset stomach, or make you lose your breath, or give you cold sore, or make you not sleep at night. I'm talking about the foods that your body feels nurtured by. Not your brain. Not your mouth. But your body.

As a writer, you should be used to lots of voices already in your head. As part of the road to health, you're going to have to learn to listen to a couple of more.

Aversion Therapy

For me, once I made the association between eating grain and feeling awful, aversion therapy kicked in.

Mouth: But those corn chips look so good! And they smell good too! Just have a few.

Brain: And twenty minutes from now, you're going to have to take an antihistamine. Your eyes are going to be running. Your throat will be scratchy. Do you even have a tissue you can use to blow your nose with?

Body: Ugh. No corn chips.

After a while, I stopped craving the foods that made me sick. As I said, for me, aversion therapy works.

That's not to say I don't still get cravings for things. Like rice. I discovered, however, that bread, even a really good artisan bread, tastes like cardboard once I hadn't had it for a year. Bread is merely a delivery device for other foods, like butter and garlic. Or jam.

I will note that aversion therapy, even for me, isn't as effective when it takes hours between the behavior and the awfulness. For example, I've discovered that I really can't tolerate a lot of dairy: some butter now and again, or even some ghee, won't bother me. Having a large piece of cheese will give me a migraine about two hours later. Eggs will give me hives in twenty minutes.

Side Note

This is the second side note that's going to ask you: what are you currently doing that you know isn't healthy for you? Why are you doing it? What needs to happen for you to be able to stop?

As I said, aversion therapy works for me. It doesn't work for everyone. Food is personal.

Just as every writer's process is different, so is every body. Your diet should be as individual as your writing.

I will advocate that you eat a lot of vegetables. However, I am aware that not all bodies can tolerate them. You may need to find a lot of workarounds to get more healthy greens in your life.

Perhaps your anti-stodgy campaign could include trying small samples of new vegetables, or new ways to cook them. A friend of mine recently discovered that the way I cooked certain vegetables made them actually taste good! (In part, it was because I didn't overcook the vegetables, unlike what she'd eaten growing up.)

Support

I was very lucky that I was able to find the website Mark's Daily Apple (www.marksdailyapple.com) back in 2009 when I eliminated all grains. This was (and continues to be!) a great resource for me. I love the success stories every Friday.

When you decide that you want to eat healthier, live healthier, make the change, you are going to need support.

I am a very independent person. I'm a functioning introvert, but I'm very much an introvert. I fool people all the time with that: they think I'm not an introvert because I'm so friendly. It has nothing to do with introversion. It's just that I'm not a shy person.

However, being in a large crowd for a long while exhausts me. There's construction going on outside my house right now, and that noise really grates on me.

I function best when I'm completely alone about eighty percent of the time. (Yes, you read that right. 80%.) Then, the other twenty percent of the time, I actively want to be with people.

Yet, even I need support. I need support from my lovely husband, from my friends, from my fellow writers, as well as a few websites that I feel support me. (As long as everyone goes away later.)

Side Note

Meditation: Who doesn't support your writing? What can you do to avoid them?

Yes, I am married. I am the most lucky person in the world. I found and was able to marry the love of my life, my true partner.

However.

Just because I married the man doesn't mean I ever have to live with him.

Usually, when I talk about this with people, the women nod their heads and the men look confused.

Meditation: How much alone time do you need? If you could, would you spend the day alone? The night alone? The week alone?

Leveling Up Your Life

One other website that I would recommend for writers: Nerdfitness.com.

The forums on the site are great. It's a built-in cheering squad for those who have decided to make changes and to try to be healthier.

One of the sayings that I've adopted from the site: What are you doing to level up your life?

If you're a gamer or even if you just sometimes play games on your phones, you understand the concept of levels. You are always trying to get to the next level in the game, to improve your score.

Your life is much more important than a game. What are you doing to get to the next level?

CHAPTER FOUR

To riff off the concept of "leveling up", one of the next things I did with the writing was to teach myself how to write while standing up.

Mind you, I was still handwriting everything at that point. So I started off learning how to write longhand standing up, then switched over to typing standing up.

Like all new things, I was uncomfortable at first. It wasn't easy. But I knew that standing would have great health benefits, so I did it anyway.

Things that made it easier for me:

1. I quickly learned that a fast scene was so much easier to write standing up.

2. Then there were the slower, more intimate scenes that generally had conversations in them. I still, to this day, will frequently sit down to write those scenes.

3. A good standing mat.

The last became essential to how comfortable I was standing. I have a topo mat. (http://ergodriven.com/topo/) I cannot recommend it highly enough. It's a wonderful mat. They used to have a more fun video on the website about all the. different positions you could assume while on a topo mat. They've now put up the video that was part of their Kickstarter campaign. While it's more informative, it isn't as much fun.

But as they say in the video, if you move while you stand, you'll assume better posture, and you'll be more energized at the end of the day.

One of the counterintuitive things that I experienced happened around taking breaks after I'd started standing.

I'd originally assumed that okay, I've been standing for fifty-five minutes. I should go sit down now.

I found that if, instead, I went and walked one thousand steps after standing for an hour, I felt better and was able to go back to work.

One of the sayings that I've had regarding my writing for a long time is: if the body is moving, the words are flowing. That is the case with me. If I sit still for too long, not only does my body get stiff, but my mind as well. (Or maybe I'm just hyper. You never know.)

So now you have a couple of things to help you level up the physicality of your writing:

- Take breaks
- Teach yourself to stand while writing

So let's delve into each of these a little more.

What To Do

You've set your timer. You've done your words. You even broke off writing in the middle of a sentence to help you get back into the flow after your break.

Now what?

I recommend finding three to four arm/wrist/hand stretches that help you, make you feel better, and do those. Every break. For me, that means every twenty minutes, as well as every fifty-five minutes. (How often you take a break may be different. Maybe you need to break every ten minutes. I know a writer who does that, and he's much younger than I am. Maybe you need to break every thirty minutes, then take your longer break after ninety minutes. I know another writer who does that. He also wears wrist braces when he types to help support his writing habit.)

Find the stretches that work for you right now. Your body changes, and hopefully, after you've developed more healthy writing habits, you're going to have to find more challenging stretches.

For me, when I am in flow state, I currently write between 2000-2200 words per hour. (I will talk more about how to do this in a healthy manner in later chapters.) Those stretches are *crucial* for me if I'm going to work for six to eight hours a day.

Even if your production rate isn't as high as mine, you still need to get in the habit of stretching when you take breaks.

Then for the longer breaks, I add in two or three stretches of my legs, and I go walk.

My goal is always: one thousand words per hour, plus one thousand steps per hour.

Side Note

Other writers ask me how I manage that production rate.

I go back to the runners. You don't just start out running five miles the first time you go running.

You also don't start out writing 2000 words per hour the first time you start writing.

You need to build to it.

Remember, writing is a muscle. It atrophies if you don't use it, just as it grows stronger the more you do use it.

Question: how can you strengthen your writing muscles? What one, specific, measurable thing can you do?

That word—measurable—is an really important concept. You can't just say, "I'm a gonna write more!" You have to say something like: I will write 500 words this week. Or: I will write two sentences on my novel every day.

The Bad Days

Not all days are created equal. There are days, even for me, that are not filled with thousands of words and steps.

What do you do on the bad days?

I don't mean the days when I'm feeling sluggish and it's going to take me a couple hours to shift my lazy butt over to the keyboard.

I mean the days when I have a migraine, or even a severe headache. Or maybe I ate something I shouldn't have and I have a horrible stomach ache.

I have tried to write anyway on those days. For me, that ended up being a mistake. The novel that I wrote despite the migraines turned out to be a copyeditor's nightmare. I repeated words, phrases, hell, whole paragraphs. My copyedit turned into a pretty harsh line edit.

Fortunately, the plot was pretty straight forward, so I didn't have to worry about that. But I ended up rewriting entire scenes because the action was so unclear. (Let me put it this way: when I got the copyedit back and went through some of those scenes, even I couldn't figure out what I meant.)

I don't know if this will be your experience or not. It may be. It may not be. You may want to experiment and see when you actually can and cannot write, not when the lazy mind says, "I'm tired! I don't wanna!" as opposed to the body saying, "I've been hanging sheetrock all day. There are no words."

This is next most important concept when it comes to being healthy:

Forgive yourself for the bad days. Be gentle with yourself instead.

Easier said than done, right?

I learned in my early thirties how important it was to forgive myself for the mistakes I'd made. Given my family of origin, that's never been easy. But it was essential for me, my health, and my writing, to learn how to be gentle with myself despite my failings.

Something that helped me down this path: What I called the *reality check*. I tried to look at my life, or what had just happened, and figure out what was real versus what I'd imagined.

I still fail frequently in social settings. I don't say something when I should, or I say something I shouldn't, or I don't notice something. Failing in a social setting is the hardest thing for me to forgive myself for.

What I've learned is to ask myself: how bad was it really? Did you just break someone's heart or merely disappoint them? Can you apologize and improve the next time? Did you just cause WWIII or merely hurt someone's feelings?

You will need to find your own path to forgive yourself for failing, for the bad days, for the sick times. No one else will forgive you for those sins. You need to figure out how to do it yourself.

Side Note

Question: How you do deal with the lazy times?

There are times when I'm not sick, or too stressed, or what have you, when I can physically write, when there are words, but I'm just not motivated to write.

I will touch on this again in a later chapter. For now, I want you to start thinking of how you can overcome these times. How do you motivate yourself?

I know another writer who says that she works for the toughest boss in the world, who won't ever let her quit.

That has never worked for me. In part, it's because I'm such an introvert, and even though the boss is me and in my head, it still feels as though I'm giving too much control to someone else.

Instead, I focus on weekly goals. Daily goals have never made sense to me. I never know when I'm going to have a bad day and I can't physically write.

Instead, I have a weekly goal. Unless I have several bad days in a row, I can make my weekly goal.

And that goal drives me to the keyboard even when I'm feeling lazy and uninspired.

So again—I want you to start developing strategies for how you will motivate yourself.

CHAPTER FIVE

The next jump in the health timeline is up to 2015. I was getting married to the love of my life. I'd quit the dayj ob and was writing full time. I was getting a good handle on *how* to write full time. I was happy and life was good.

I was also stressed. It was June, and we were getting married in July. I was in the process of finishing up my wedding dress. I'd already made his wedding shirt and vest. We were doing so many things for the wedding ourselves, from making all the wine and mead, to canning jam as presents for the guests to take home, etc.

We went camping in June with a great group of writers. (We go camping with this group every year. It's kind of a writing retreat, set up with two different areas in the campground. One has power and is covered and is a quiet area where you're expected to sit down, shut up, and write. The other is the social area.)

However, due to my diet, I had to do most of the cooking for the weekend ahead of time. I didn't expect anyone else to accommodate me and how I ate. So a bit more stress.

I think it was the second day we were there, I got a migraine.

No problem. Maybe I got overheated and was dehydrated. I wasn't sure, but that sounded good. So I took a Maxalt, laid down and slept in the tent for a while.

But the headache didn't really go away. Not fully. This was kind of strange. However, I also figured I was stressed, and that the headache would go away eventually.

It didn't. Instead, by the next day, I had another migraine.

I ended up having seven migraines over the next twelve days. Heads plitting, I can't think, types of migraines.

WTH?

It had to be an abnormality. The pills weren't doing their job like they had been, though. (Due to my insurance company, I'd had to switch from the name-brand migraine medication I'd been on decades and go to a generic.)

I went to see my naturopath. I happened to mention that while my wheat allergy had died down tremendously, my corn allergy was still off the charts. Whenever I was exposed to corn starch in gravy or something, my allergic reaction went off the charts.

He hadn't realized that I was specifically allergic to corn.

The thyroid medication that I'd been taking for so long had corn starch in it.

That was when I learned that corn starch is in EVERYTHING.

Did you know that they coat paper plates in corn starch so they don't stick together? Same with plastic forks and spoons.

It's also in aspirin. Most generic versions of drugs like acetaminophen and ibuprofen. It's in my antihistamines. Everything.

I don't believe in a single cause for things. However, I do believe that part of why I suddenly started having so many migraines is because I'd overdosed on corn.

I went from having zero to three migraines a month to suddenly, seemingly overnight, having twelve to fifteen migraines a month. Even after I'd eliminated the corn from my diet, the migraines raged on.

Side Note

Meditation: what would you do if you suddenly lost half of your available time to do anything?

The migraines didn't care if I was planning on writing or doing publishing work. Plus, the most cruel aspect was that a symptom of an oncoming migraine was that I'd lose the ability to focus. Even if I wanted to work, and forced myself to at least get something done, I couldn't do what I normally did.

So even if it was a month with fewer migraines, I still ended up losing half the month.

What would you do if you suddenly lost half your life?

Eliminating the Obvious

I saw a neurologist for the migraines, and had an MRI done to make sure I wasn't suffering from some sort of tumor.

Nothing obvious, though.

So I started digging in and trying to find the not obvious. I had a pretty healthy diet. What was I missing?

I also tried more drugs. I tried a different migraine medication that actually worked better. I discovered that the generic version of my old migraine medication contained corn starch, which is probably why it wasn't as effective as it had been. I cleaned up my diet some more.

I exercised when I could. I know that one of the pieces of advice that people always give is to exercise when you have a migraine.

At that point, even doing the mildest walking would cause the migraine to become more intense and last longer. (I will talk more about this later.)

Two Breakthroughs

At one point, I'd discovered Dr. Terry Wahls.

Dr. Terry Wahls has multiple sclerosis, or MS. The pills and traditional treatments were leaving her sicker and sicker. As she's a medical doctor, she finally decided to take matters into her own hands.

She developed the initial Wahls protocol diet. By following this diet, she was able to reverse her MS. There are now hundreds of thousands of people who suffer from MS and other autoimmune diseases who follow her protocol diet and have found the same success.

But I'm getting ahead of myself.

I discovered the initial Wahls protocol years before. I'd even followed it for a while. It starts with nine cups of vegetables a day: two cups each of three very specific types of vegetables.

I felt fantastic when I was on the Wahls protocol. I'd seriously never felt better in my life.

However, nine cups of vegetables was just too much. I couldn't maintain it. I discovered that anything less than eight didn't have the same effect.

But I always remembered how good I felt on that diet, and always said that when I got rich, I was going to hire a personal chef who would get me all those good veggies.

While I was teaching a workshop (and having massive migraines every single day) I discovered that two of the people taking the workshop were on the Wahls protocol.

That was when I learned that Dr. Wahls had developed three levels of the protocol. Level three only required six cups of veggies per day.

I had always known there was a connection between food and health.

A few weeks after the workshop finished, I committed to trying level three of the Wahls protocol, also known as Wahls Paleo Plus.

Side Note

For some people, the best way for them to make changes is through baby steps. Basically, baby step + baby step + baby step = big step.

For other people, they're the rip the bandage off all at once type. They won't necessarily succeed at taking small steps. They need to take a huge leap, all at once, in order to succeed.

As for me, I'm somewhere in between. I tend to take a largish leap at first, land, make myself comfortable, then start making smaller adjustments.

Question: what is the best way for you to make changes to your life? Do you need to break everything down and take small steps? Or do you need to make a huge leap of faith? What works for you?

The next question is just as important: What will work for you in terms of stopping unhealthy behaviors? Small steps? Giant leap? Something in between?

Ketogenic Diet

The diet that I'm currently following is a ketogenic diet. Basically, it's a high fat, medium protein, low carb diet.

And did I mention six cups of veggies every day?

At the same time I started the diet, I eliminated some other things from my diet as a test:

- Eggs
- Dairy
- Nightshades

Why?

I suspected that I'd always been allergic to eggs. I didn't want to be allergic to dairy, however, people who are allergic to eggs also tend to be allergic to the same animal protein that's also found in dairy.

As for nightshades, I'd always known that eggplant was deadly for me. Within twenty minutes of eating something with eggplant in it, I'd end up with sores all over the inside of my mouth as well as covering my lips. Too many tomatoes would have the same effect. As far as I knew, I didn't really react to peppers and potatoes. This is typical of nightshades, BTW. Most people can be deathly allergic to one part of the family and still be able to eat the others.

For the time being, I decided to just eliminate them all.

The results were mixed.

I didn't decrease the frequency of my migraines in the least.

However, the pain went down significantly.

I must have still been doing something wrong, though.

But what?

CHAPTER SIX

I'm returning to the concept of "leveling up" your writing.

There are two concepts I'm going to introduce in this chapter. They may seem to contradict each other, but they don't. Instead, they really compliment each other. Learning how to use both of these techniques will really help your ability to write.

The two techniques are:

- Reaching flow state
- Cycling

Critical vs. Creative Voice

I've talked about critical vs. creative voice before in *Business for Breakfast, Volume 4: The Intermediate Storyteller*. I'm going to recap here, but if you want more detail, go there.

Your creative voice is your inner two year old who wants to strip off all her clothes, go running outside, and then play naked in the street.

As an artist, you take risks. That's a lot of what that creative voice is all about. It's about exposing yourself, being true as an artist, being honest with yourself.

Your critical voice is the voice of the parent, or the teacher, or even society at large, which says, "No, don't do that."

Your critical voice is responsible for keeping you safe.

Safe art is, well, quite frankly, boring.

When you write, you need to be in creative voice. You are unique, and you are the only one who can tell your stories.

But that critical voice is going to pop up and tell you, "No. Don't write that. That's boring," or "You can't say that! Everyone will know!" or even, "You know girls can't write science fiction. Why are you even trying?"

Critical voice will kill your writing and drive you away from the keyboard. A lot of critical voice comes about from fear. You're going to have to deal with your fears.

How do you help get over being paralyzed by your critical voice?

One of the methods is by learning how to always enter flow state when you start writing.

Flow State

What exactly do I mean by flow state? It's actually a psychological term, when you're fully immersed in the writing and the words are coming directly to your fingers without you really having to think about them. Sometimes, flow state is referred to as being *in the zone*.

What does this have to do with critical and creative voice?

If you're *in the zone*, critical voice is no longer present. You're playing, the writing is fun and easy, the words are flowing.

How do you teach yourself to always reach flow state every time you sit down to write?

Again, as with most writing, reaching flow state automatically means exercising that writing muscle consistently. It isn't going to happen the first time you sit down to start writing. It takes practice.

You can get there. You can do this.

How?

One of the resources I recommend is a book by Chris Fox, *5000*

Words an Hour. I disagree with some of what he says. (I disagree with some of what most anyone says—it's that artist/contrarian in me.) For example, keeping the spreadsheets he recommends would annoy the hell out of me. Other writer swear by them. It's your process. What works for you?

He talks a lot about flow state. He approaches it differently than I do, and he advocates a different writing process than I do.

However, the starting point is the same: every time you sit down to write, you just start writing.

Start Small

Chris Fox recommends starting with a five minute writing sprint. I agree. He has a lot of very good advice about clearing the decks before you start writing, so that all you'll do is just sit down and write.

So for your first sprint, you're going to set a timer and sit down to write for five minutes.

That's it.

No rewriting. No stopping to fix a word. Just write. Focus, and write.

As soon as you finish that first sprint, I want you to stand up and walk away from the computer. Don't fill in your spreadsheets or check your email or hop onto Facebook "just for a minute" (that somehow turns into three hours).

Walk away from your computer.

I know, that story is still eating at you. Or maybe it's that misspelled word. But you're in training right now, not running the actual marathon.

Walk away from the computer.

This is part of the necessary training that you need for teaching yourself to take breaks.

When you're ready for your next five minute sprint, clear the decks like you did before, start your timer, and begin writing.

Write. Don't do anything but put words onto the page for five minutes.

Then walk away again.

Everyctime you sit down to the computer, write. Write quickly. Don't think. Don't rewrite. Don't play games or check your email. Just write.

The Goal

What you are aiming for, eventually, is not to just type words, but to write, really write, everyctime you sit down at your writing computer.

I don't want you to start getting sloppy, however. The goal of the writing sprints is to get you to the computer, and to get you writing. It is *not* to get you to write a bad, broken first draft. You need to write. The writing sprint will teach you to always write when you sit down (or stand up, or get on your unicycle, what have you.)

Rewriting

You may end up hating everything that you write in your writing sprints. That's okay. This is just practice, exercise. You may or may not want to include it as a performance piece.

Chris Fox advocates editing sprints as well, after you finish writing, to go back and fix all those things that need fixing.

I'm not sure about that. There are some things, like misspelled words, that you should fix.

Anything else?

Writers are notoriously bad when it comes to judging the quality of their work. I know New York Times bestsellers who are convinced to this day that everything they write sucks.

After you write that first piece, you may want to hand it to a first reader (NOT a critique group) and see what they think.

DO NOT tell them how quickly you wrote it, or that it's just a practice piece. Let them tell you whether it works or not.

If they don't understand something, or it isn't clear, and you agree with their assessment, then maybe you can make some changes.

If they tell you, "I really liked the character" or "the world building is so cool!" or something like that, WRITE THAT DOWN.

Really.

You won't hear it. You won't believe it. You need to write down the compliments that people give you about your writing so that you won't mess with what's working.

Cycling

By now, you've completed some writing sprints. You feel more confident that you'll actually get to the page on a regular basis.

Let's consider cycling, as the second technique to level up your writing.

Basically, cycling is going back either a section, possibly back to the start of a chapter, and reading what you've done to get you back into the writing flow.

"But wait! Haven't I been practicing getting into writing flow? Why should I cycle?"

This is an excellent question.

For me, I end up doing a bit of both. If it's been a day or more since I've written, I'll cycle back either to the start of a scene, or to the start of the chapter, and read through it.

I am NOT editing at this point. I'm not looking at the words and hating what I've been doing. I do not let critical voice into the room. Instead, I'm getting myself back into the story, refinding my creative voice.

Doesn't this go against flow state?

No, it doesn't. There are nuances here that I'm going to try to explain.

Flow state means being in that creative spot where you're writing. It doesn't mean you're always writing as fast and as furiously as you possibly can. It means the words and ideas are flowing. It doesn't mean you're writing crappy first drafts.

After you've trained yourself to always sit down and just write, you can start expanding your writing to include cycling.

Flow state is about getting yourself to the keyboard and creating.

Cycling is a method for creating.

I would rather take the time cycling, and fixing things as they come up, rather than having to do an editing sprint through the entire piece. I want to have touched every part of the novel more than once while writing rather than editing.

I went to a writing retreat in May, 2017. I wrote a 52,000 word novel in five days—so basically, 10,000 words a day. I also walked 10,000 steps a day. (I will go into this level of marathoning in a later chapter.)

Did I hit flow state every time I sat down (or stood up) to write? Absolutely.

Did I also cycle? Improve the beginning (which are always the roughest part for me, according to more than one first reader)? Absolutely.

So again, flow state is to teach yourself to sit down, shut up, and write.

Cycling makes that work clean by the time you're finished with it.

Side Note

A lot of writers advocate knowing what you are writing before you start. I tried that for a while. I would sit down for five minutes with pen and paper and write about the chapter or scene I was starting. I let my excitement build so that I was all primed to start writing.

I found after a while that I was resenting that extra time. It felt unnatural to me to plan that way. I wanted to sit down and write! Not plan what I was writing.

For me, I've found that training myself to be in flow state every time I sit down to write is much more effective as well as more natural than planning out what I'm writing. Planning out what I was about to write before I wrote was a crutch.

Meditation: What is the natural way for you to write your current project? Planning? Or writing into the darkness? Remember, whatever method you're using for this project may change for the next project.

CHAPTER SEVEN

When last we left our intrepid writer, she'd changed her diet, but her migraines hadn't stopped.

This was when luck stepped in and said, "Here. Let me show you the way."

For the last couple of years, there's been something called, *The World Migraine Summit*. Basically, it's a group of experts (doctors, nurses, scientists) who have been interviewed regarding their work on migraines and headaches. The interviews are recorded throughout the year. Then during the summit, they are available online.

If you sign up for the summit beforehand, you get access to each day's interviews when they go live. The free access only gives you twenty-four hour access. There are also live talks at the beginning and the end of the summit.

The summit was happening right at this time. Luck.

There were a few talks that interested me as part of the 2017 lineup. One was by Dr. Josh Turkette (generally referred to as Dr. T.) His talk was on using the paleo diet to cure your migraines.

As I was already on a paleo diet, had been since 2009, this talk made me curious.

It turned out to be the missing piece for me.

Scammy Name Is Not A Scam

Dr. T proclaimed his process, "The Migraine Miracle." The website is, http://www.mymigrainemiracle.com.

Seriously?

I figure a bunch of people who need this information are turned off by the name. I nearly was. However, I'd already listened to Dr. T talk about how diet can cure your migraines. His theory is that the hypothalamus, which is responsible for regulating your brain, gets over stimulated by the shifts in blood sugar caused by the standard American diet (also known as SAD).

This made sense to me. I already knew that sugar was the culprit behind a lot of my headaches.

But sugar, and those shifts in blood sugar, were a month or so behind me. There had to be something else.

That was when I learned about rebound headaches.

Basically, rebound headaches are caused by regular, long-term use of your regular migraine meds.

Dr. T has a page about how to figure out if you're in rebound or not. He lists seven key identifiers.

I had seven out of seven.

Well, shit.

I wasn't actually having migraines anymore. I was just rebounding. In fact, I probably still only had 2-3 migraines per month, and the rest were just rebound headaches.

The cure?

Stop taking medication, not just my lovely Maxalt, but all over the counter meds as well, like Excedrin and NyQuil, which I'd come to rely on.

Ugh.

It took me a month to wean myself away from everything. The only reason why I kept going wasn't just because I'm a touch stubborn, but because what Dr. T said about how to cure your migraines actually worked for me.

And I still think it's the weirdest thing in the world.

I've had migraines since I was eighteen years old. I took medication for them regularly.

Now, in order to get rid of my migraines, I'm supposed to fast, breathe deeply, do mild exercise, meditate, and drink water with salt in it? You're joking, right?

But it worked. The first migraine I "treated" in this manner disappeared after a few hours as if it had never been there.

Again, weirdest thing in the world. I was so used to what I referred to as my "migraine hangover," that time after the migraine was over when I was dealing with the after effects of the drugs.

Instead, the pain is gone, I can think again, and just move on with my day.

Okay, I can almost understand why you'd call that a migraine miracle. I really can. It's still a scammy name. But it works.

Side Note

If you suffer from migraines, go and get Dr. T's book, *The Migraine Miracle*.

Go and read about migraines on his website. https://www.mymigrainemiracle.com/

Possibly join the Facebook group. Now, I have issues with the Facebook group. (Come on, you know I'm going to have issues with some of this.) Dr. T and his wife run the group and are very strict about what you can post. I personally think that the Wahls Paleo Protocol is one of the best ketogenic diets that's out there. It's a nutritionally dense ketogenic (keto) diet, not something all keto diets can claim.

However, Dr. T's wife won't let me post about it on their group. Fair enough. They sell a meal plan with recipes, etc. They don't want the competition. It is their site.

So join the Facebook group if you want, but realize that you won't get a lot of new information from there. Once you've read the book and the website, you pretty much have all the information you need to enact your own migraine miracle.

Exercise

Most doctors, and frequently other migraine sufferers, will tell you that doing mild exercise while you have a migraine will help.

I call bullshit.

If I tried to exercise or walk while I had a migraine, it just made it worse. The pain would increase and the headache would last longer.

It wasn't until I started getting a handle on my migraines that any sort of exercise would help.

It still must be very mild. I do what I call, *mindful walking* when I'm in pain. Basically, I walk slowly while breathing deeply. I am conscious with every step that I continue to breathe.

Salt

As you may or may not already know, the recommended daily allowance (RDA) for food was developed for white males.

If you are not a white male, your requirements may be different.

As a woman, I actually require *more* salt than the RDA says I should have.

What I've learned, is that as someone who suffers from migraines, I require **even more** salt.

In addition, I make all of my own food. I eat very, very little packaged or processed food. Guess what? If I don't add salt to my food, I don't get any.

I have now developed the habit of always salting my water. I don't put in enough for me to be able to taste it. But I always have salt in my water, and I try to add salt to my food. (My mom had hypertension, so I learned to cook without ever adding salt to anything.)

If you suffer from migraines, salt could be key to your curing your migraines. It certainly was for me. I can now tell when I've had enough salt the day before versus when I haven't.

Heat

Being a woman of a certain age, I suffer from hot flashes now and again. And guess what? I get migraines after I have a hot flash.

If Dr. T's theory of why we get migraines in correct, this suddenly makes sense. If your hypothalamus is over stimulated by blood sugar, it can also get over stimulated by heat.

Most people who suffer from migraines already know this. If you get too hot, you are increasing your chances of a migraine starting.

They tell women my age to start layering, so that you can discard layers in public if necessary. If you have migraines, you need to start doing the same thing. Make sure that you can get yourself cooled off if you feel yourself start to overheat.

Side Note

Meditation: teaching yourself patience. How can you learn to be more patient? Me, I want to be fixed NOW.

What I've learned is that healing is a slow process. Once I stopped all the medication, I knew it was still going to take four to six months for my brain to heal from the constant migraines.

It's so disappointing when you have yet another migraine when you thought you were healed, were getting better.

I advise getting yourself a calendar where you can track your migraines and headache days.

For me, I ended up using two apps on my phone: Migraine Buddy for the migraines, and Universal Diary for keeping track of the diet.

My progress was slow. And it was difficult to see that I was, in fact, making progress when I felt so crummy.

But looking back, I can see that I was.

I'm at the far end, now. A single migraine in a month, as well as just a single headache day.

It's possible. You can do it. But you will have to be patient.

CHAPTER EIGHT

In small ways, then in larger ways, I used marathoning to help improve my writing.

What exactly do I mean by marathoning?

It means taking a day, or a weekend, or possibly a week, and not doing anything but write the entire time.

In order to survive that level of intense physical activity (because remember, writing is a physical activity) I had to have all my healthy habits in place first: an ergonomic place where I did write, standing so I didn't hurt my back, stretching regularly, flow state and cycling.

At first, my husband and I did small marathons, where we'd just write during a long weekend, say, over labor day weekend, or maybe even over Thanksgiving weekend (as it was just the two of us and no family to go visit).

We also did what is known as CampCon. Every June, a group of writers gets together at a Mount Hood campsite in north central Oregon. The campsite is set up with two areas: one has power and cover, the other generally has a warm fire pit and lots of chairs around it. In the first area, the expectation is that you will shut up and write. The other area is where you socialize.

My husband and I treat CampCon as a marathon, and try to get as many words as possible done over the course of three-four days. It's fun writing with all those other people, all focused on doing the same task.

The Big Marathon

In May 2017, I went on a writer's retreat with the express intention of writing a novel in a week. I'd never done it before, so I had no idea if I could. I was also not as healthy, so I was dealing with severe headaches for more than one day.

The writing retreat happened at a beach house on the Oregon coast. I went there with four other writers, all women. The location was gorgeous, overlooking the ocean, and the weather cooperated after the first couple of days and was sunny.

While the novel I was writing was brand new, it was the third in a trilogy. I already knew the characters and the world.

I don't generally outline my novels. I will occasionally. However, the outlines I write tend to be short, and not very specific. The shortest outline I wrote was 125 words long. The novel was written from two points of view. While the action that occurred for both characters was completely different, I wanted their emotional arc to be the same, and that was what the "outline" was.

What I will find before I start writing a novel are what I call the touch points—the key turning points of the story, whether they're emotional or plot driven, or both.

To prepare for the marathon, I reread the first two novels. I'd written them both over a year before I wrote the third one. That gave me some ideas of where I wanted the third one to go, some of the touch points.

Then, to get to the writing retreat, I had a long, five hour drive. I set up my phone to take voice dictation, and I basically brainstormed the entire drive down. (I don't know about you, but I always find a long-distance trip inspirational.)

By the time I reached the beach house, I had a two of the four major touch points for the novel. I also had what I ended up calling points of interest.

Imagine a large map that contains points of interest scattered across it. Maybe two dozen in all.

While I'm writing the novel, I know that I need to visit all of those points of interest. Plus, there will be other places that I'll discover in the process of writing the novel that I'll need to get to.

However, this "map" contains no topography. I had no idea if I was going to be climbing a mountain to get to a point, or swimming across a lake, or walking down the street of a city. I also had no idea of the order in which I had to visit all those points.

I just started writing.

The first day, after driving for five hours, I wrote 2000 words, just to get my feet wet.

I knew that if I waited to write until the next day, I'd start worrying. Panic might even set it. Instead, I just jumped in. I figured if all those words sucked, I could just throw them out and start fresh.

The next morning, I followed my usual routine: get up, stretch and do yoga, take a shower, eat breakfast, check my email to see if there's an emergency I need to deal with (but not actually write or reply to any email) then go write.

Because I'd immersed myself in the world earlier, and as I had a couple thousand words already written, it was pretty easy for me to cycle back over what I'd written and then start.

The Wall

That first day, I was a little surprised at how easy it seemed to be going. I was in flow state. I was getting in my stretches, so my hands and arms weren't bothering me. I was getting up every hour and walking a thousand steps.

Then, I started slowing down. The words weren't flowing. I wasn't sure what the next scene was. My brain seemed to be shutting down.

Crap. Was I getting sick? Had I reached the end? I wasn't anywhere near my goal of 10,000 words for the day. I was only around 6000 words. But I felt as though I'd really hit the wall.

So I took my lunch break, a long two hour break. I relaxed and talked with the other writers at the retreat. I made myself some more coffee. I checked my email and replied to a few things.

By the time I got back to the computer, I was ready to write again, and I managed the rest of my words.

That happened every day. At first, it was right between 5-6000 words. Then it started happening between 6-7000. By the last day, I didn't hit the wall until close to 8000 words.

I believe this is part of the "writing is a muscle" phenomenon. I could do 6000 words in one morning because that's how strong my storytelling/writing muscle was. As I kept stretching it, it got stronger.

The Experience

Normally, when I'm writing a novel, when I go to sleep at night I'm thinking about the novel. When I wake up and am just lazing in bed before I get up, I'm thinking about the novel. At odd times during the day, someone will say something and I'll go, "Oh! That goes into the novel."

This experience was different. I didn't find myself thinking about the novel at odd times, or in the mornings or the evenings. I was so immersed in the story, it didn't rise up to conscious levels. I just sat down and started writing. My back brain was working furiously, however, as more than one reader has told me that the third novel is very satisfying.

There were a couple of other things that I did differently as well.

Since this was a straightforward story, all from one character's point of view, I didn't bother with chapters. I just put in scene breaks, and after I finished, I went back and broke the story up into chapters.

I discovered that I'd gotten into the habit of taking breaks when I reached the end of a scene or the end of a chapter. As I had too many words to write, I wasn't going to "cheat" and take my break early. Instead, I'd write, and write hard, up to the moment my timer went off.

Then I'd break hard. Whether that was in the middle of a sentence or not.

I stopped watching my word count. Prior to this, I was always very concerned with my word count per hour. I wanted to make sure I was getting in my words.

About mid-way through the week, I realized I'd speeded up.

Before that time, I was writing between 1000-1500 words per hour.

I was writing faster than that. I had reached total flow stage. And I was writing 2000 words per hour.

Watching my word count freaked me out. I had no idea that I could write that many words in an hour. So I just paid attention to how many words I was at for the day, not for the hour.

Because I'd set the hard deadline of 10,000 words per day, once I reached that, my brain kind of shut down every day. I believe if I'd been able to tell myself, 11,000 words per day after the third day, I probably would have written that much.

But I generally hit a wall every day around 10,000 words. I was done. And I was kind of fried for a while afterward. There just wasn't much brain left after doing that kind of work.

Earlier in the week, I'd have another writing session after dinner, so I could get in my 10,000 words.

By later in the week, I was finishing my 10,000 words by mid-afternoon. I tried to have an evening session after that, but my brain wasn't having anything to do with that. I was done.

Aftermath

After I finished writing a novel in a week, and I drove the five hours back home, I found I needed a day or so to recover. I was tired, physically and mentally.

However, after I took a day off, I found I could write again.

I also discovered that I'd reached a new level of productivity and output. I wasn't always able to achieve 2000 words an hour—I think I need to be immersed to reach that.

But I'd reached a new level of storytelling. I'd never been able to write a short story in a single day. Even if the story wasn't that many words, it still took me two to three days to write.

I could now suddenly write short stories in a single day.

I also found that flow state was really easy to achieve, if I was working on the right project. If I was working on the wrong project, I couldn't achieve flow state at all. It was really obvious.

I plan on doing another marathon in October, 2017. This time, I have a 60,000 word novel to write, which I plan on doing in six days. Wish me luck!

CHAPTER NINE

I haven't talked a lot about the food aspects of being healthy. I personally follow a diet that's kind of at one extreme. I start with six cups of vegetables every day. I do not eat grains, soy, eggs, or dairy. My husband and I joke that all I eat are dead critter and fresh veggies.

As I've said before, the diet I follow is not the right diet for every body. What I need to be healthy is different than what your body needs.

However, there are some commonalities among diets that tend to be healthier.

Start Reading Ingredient Labels

Just as you wouldn't merely click through the terms of service (TOS) on a website, you shouldn't pick anything up from the grocery store that contains a bunch of chemicals and not food. This is basically the advice you see elsewhere: If you can't pronounce it, don't eat it.

NOTE: You *are* reading every TOS you come across, right? If you are not, your assignment is to go find the Facebook TOS and read them. They're written in pretty clear language.

Including the part where they claim that ALL the intellectual property (IP) that you post on their site is now owned by them.

If you haven't read that TOS, do so right now. And then never, ever, *ever* post snippets from your work in progress on Facebook ever again. You can post them on your website and link to the website from Facebook, but don't put original IP up on Facebook.

Pretty please?

I find the disconnect between the brand name and the ingredients frequently hilarious. Particularly on items that claim things like, "Just like Grandma used to make!"

Then you look at the ingredient list, and it contains chemicals that I can't even pronounce. Now, maybe if Grandma had a PhD in chemistry, she might have followed this recipe. I doubt it, however.

One of the healthiest things you can do for yourself is to start reading ingredient lists, and cut out the chemicals. Grandma would thank you.

Natural Flavorings

The Federal Drug Administration (FDA) had no definition for the word "*natural*". So any processed food can claim to be, "all natural ingredients!" and no one can sue them for it, even if half the items on the ingredient list are merely chemicals.

This goes double for anything under the heading, "natural flavorings." The FDA defines natural flavorings as any item that was at one point derived from nature. This means that any and all chemicals and processes can be added to that once natural thing. So that natural flavoring might contain one percent something you'd recognized, that's then been processed, churned, and "enhanced" with a bunch of chemicals.

Food manufacturers also use the catchall natural flavorings for a host of things that you may or may not want to eat. For people who are sensitive to soy, eggs, or dairy, they need to avoid natural flavorings like the plague, because they will often contain one or more of those things.

Prep

I know, I know. You're busy juggling all the things: day job, relationship, kids, dog, and writing. Now you need to think about food prep?

This is about eating healthier. Prepackaged food, even the "natural" brands, are still not going to be good for you. There are too many chemicals, too much salt.

If you want to start including more home cooked food, one of the easiest ways to do this is to prepare some of the ingredients as well as the food ahead of time.

For a long time, I did all my cooking on Sunday afternoon. Then I reheated dishes all week, whether it was hamburgers I'd cooked out on the grill, or stew. I'd only have to cook my veggies fresh (and I'm going to get into preparing those too.)

I never make a single serving of anything. If I can, I try to always have two to three days of leftover with any meal I make. My husband jokes about me making day-old spaghetti.

Prepping—First Steps

First of all, what are you going to put your leftovers in? If you are committed to eating healthier and preparing more food in advance, I suggest spending the money on a matching set of food storage containers. Having the right size container for what you need, that are all stackable, may help you overcome some of your hesitancy.

Always get containers you can see through, so that way you don't have to open something to know what it is.

The big discount stores generally have glass containers with rubber lids that go from freezer to either microwave or oven easily.

Next, this might be the time to invest in either sharpening your knives, or getting a new set that is already sharp. Food prep is so much easier with the proper tools.

Ditto with a cutting board. My husband really likes the huge butcher-block type of cutting board we got as a wedding present. I much prefer the small thin one we have. Both will do the job. What will delight you when it comes to preparing food?

Toys! No, Wait, I mean Tools!

It's easy to go kind of nuts with all the pretty toys and expensive tools that you think you might need, but in the end, don't. These are some of the tools that you may or may not actually need, but that I have and really enjoy:

A good garlic press (the brand I have is Zyliss, and it's wonderful)

A vacuum sealer (I freeze so much food it's worth it)

A chest freezer (frequently called a coffin freezer, and come on, what writer doesn't want one of those?)

High powered blender (I make a lot of smoothies in order to get all the vegetables I need into my daily diet)

A good steamer for veggies. I recommend The Pampered Chef Small Micro Cooker. It's the easiest one I've ever found and I've used mine since 1997, so it's durable as well.

A good crockpot.

Prepping—Next Steps

So you have your accoutrement. Now you get to figure out *what* to prep.

For me, because I eat a lot of vegetables, I have a lot of pre-prep of veggies that either then go into the fridge or the freezer, so I can just grab a handful as needed.

Veggies that I prep and freeze:

Bok choy: We get one of the big ones, chop it up, throw it into the freezer to add to stir fries, soup, breakfast scrambles, what have you.

Spinach: We frequently get one of the large plastic containers of spinach, then throw it into the freezer. Ditto with kale and mustard greens. Grab a frozen handful, crush, and add to almost anything.

Avocados: Did you know that you can freeze avocados? Cut them in half, scoop them out of their skins, scoop out the nut in the center, then place the halves on a cookie sheet and pop them into the freezer. Once they're frozen solid, you can throw them all together into a plastic bag. They aren't good for salads once they've been frozen.

However, thirty seconds in the microwave defrosts them, and you can make guacamole easily. Or just throw them solid into a smoothie.

Broccoli: While I love broccoli, I honestly go through phases, where I sometimes can't keep enough in the house vs. the times I just want it for flavor. For the latter, I buy a large quantity, break it into smaller individual servings, then vacuum seal them.

Veggies that I prep and refrigerate:

Cabbage: I buy large heads of purple cabbage and cut them into smaller pieces. That way, I can just grab a handful of cabbage for salads, etc. (I like the purple cabbage because it's pretty, and because the more colorful your plate, the healthier it tends to be.) This may be too much prep for you. They also make bags of shredded cabbage that you can just buy.

Cauliflower: I find that if I have already chunked the cauliflower up into smaller pieces, I'm much more likely to add cauliflower to whatever I'm cooking. I don't rice it, though some people swear by that.

Celery: I try to buy celery that's really green, and that has a lot of leaves on it. I will cut the leaves off and stick them in a separate container, then use those for smoothies or salads. The stems I chop into small pieces, which I can use for salads or soup.

One of the veggies I don't prep are carrots. I don't buy bunches of carrots. Instead, I get the small, "baby" carrots that I can eat without any prep. I also don't prep lettuce: I buy either cartons or bags of them, depending on how I'm feeling that week.

If I've planned right, I can prepare most of my veggies on a weekend day, and have enough to last me for a week. The key here is that I need to make it as easy as possible for me to get at and eat my veggies.

Prepping Meals

As I said earlier, I always make enough so that I have leftovers. That is an easy way for me to cook ahead of time.

Another way is to prepare meals ahead of time. For example, you can put together all the ingredients you need for a crockpot meal ahead of time, freeze it, then on the day you want to use it, pull it out of the freezer, put it into the crockpot, and let it cook all day.

Similarly, you can make salads ahead of time. Look up "mason jar salads" for all the ideas you could possibly need, and then some. You can make five days of salad to take with for your lunches.

Me? I love salad in the spring and summer. Come fall and winter, I want soups and stews.

Guess what are also really easy to make ahead of time? Throw the ingredients in the crockpot and just let 'em cook all day.

Reusing

Bone broth is a big thing right now. I have always made my own stock as well as bone broth.

How do you make bone broth?

First of all, any time you have chicken, or ribs, or any other kind of meat that has a bone in it, save the bones. Put them into a gallon plastic bag in your freezer. You may or may not want to separate out the different types of meat. I tend to separate the pork from the beef or chicken. Pork bones make a very sweet broth, and it can be disconcerting if that's not what I'm going for.

When the gallon bag is half to three quarters full, you have enough! Throw the bones into your crockpot. Fill the crockpot with water. Pour in a splash of vinegar. Add a lot of salt and maybe a little spice, perhaps some garlic, ginger, rosemary, thyme, what have you. Cover and let cook for twelve to twenty four hours. Strain and enjoy!

I generally also add chicken feet to whatever broth I'm cooking. That gives it a lot more of that gelatin that you're looking for in a good bone broth.

Did you know that you can do the same with your veggies?

Instead of throwing out the ends of the celery that you don't want to eat, or the parts of your bok choy, or even the carrots skins and cabbage ends, put them all into a large gallon plastic bag in your freezer. When the bag is stuffed to the brim (and only then) empty the bag into your crockpot. Completely fill the crockpot with water. Add a lot of salt and maybe some spices. Cook for twenty-four hours.

Marathon Prepping

When I was getting ready to go down to the coast and write an insane amount, I prepared almost all the food I was going to eat that week ahead of time.

Instead of making a separate bone broth, I threw a whole chicken into the crockpot, added some salt and some garlic, a splash of vinegar and a lot of water. I cooked the whole thing for six to eight hours. Then I deboned the chicken and just took the meat and broth with me. I had lovely chicken soup every morning for breakfast, throwing in veggies as needed, as well as kelp noodles for texture.

I had pre-cooked hamburgers that I could just heat up, along with pre-cooked sausages. I had my veggies all prepped, all I had to do was throw them together. I had all the ingredients I needed to make smoothies as well.

When it came to meal time, I never had to think. All I had to do was assemble ingredients together and I'd have a meal in five minutes or less. This was very important, particularly at that time, as I didn't have a lot of brain power for anything other than the writing.

I also prepared all my snacks and treats ahead of time, such as dried apples, fat bombs, and pork rinds. That way, I would eat what I had and not be tempted by what other people were eating, such as M&Ms or popcorn.

IN CONCLUSION

There isn't a single path to health, I'm afraid. I wish it were as easy as, "Always eat these five foods to burn extra calories!"

One of the largest problems that we, the consumers, face is that the food industry is a multi-trillion dollar one. They have deep pockets, and are not afraid to pay for "research" that shows how healthy their food actually is. This is part of why it's so hard to know what you should or shouldn't eat.

This goes back to the listening. What does your body tell you is good? Again, not what your brain tells you (because it's looking for comfort) or your mouth (which is all about the yummy and not much else.) What fortifies your body? What do you find incredibly satisfying?

For me, it's always good meat and fresh veggies. But then again, by following that sort of diet, I've cured my migraines and a number of other health issues.

You're going to have to find your own path. You can do this. It will take some work. And you're going to screw up now and again.

Me—I still make choices to not adhere to my diet every day. For example, when my sweetie and I celebrated our wedding anniversary. I made the decision to not follow my usual diet. I didn't "fall off the wagon" and I didn't "eat badly"—I made a choice.

Mind you, I paid heavily for that choice the next day. But it was worth it.

IN CONCLUSION

What value is your health? What do you have to do to achieve it, and keep writing in the meanwhile?

Best of luck
Leah Cutter
Seattle, WA

READ MORE!

Be sure to pick up the other books in the Business for Breakfast series!

The Beginning Professional Writer
The Beginning Professional Publisher
The Beginning Professional Storyteller
The Intermediate Professional Storyteller
Business Planning for Professional Publishers
The Healthier Professional Writer
The Three Act Structure for Professional Writers

ABOUT THE AUTHOR

Leah Cutter writes page-turning, wildly imaginative fiction in exotic locations, such as a magical New Orleans, the ancient Orient, Hungary, the Oregon coast, rural Kentucky, Seattle, Minneapolis, and many others.

She writes literary, fantasy, mystery, science fiction, and horror fiction. Her short fiction has been published in magazines like Alfred Hitchcock's Mystery Magazine and Talebones, anthologies like Fiction River, and on the web. Her long fiction has been published both by New York publishers as well as small presses.

Find Leah's books here.

Follow her blog at www.LeahCutter.com.

Never miss a release!

If you'd like to be notified of new releases, sign up for my newsletter.

I only send out newsletters once a quarter, will never spam you, or use your email for nefarious purposes. You can also unsubscribe at any time.

http://www.leahcutter.com/newsletter/

Reviews

It's true. Reviews help me sell more books. If you've enjoyed this story, please consider leaving a review of it on your favorite site.

ABOUT KNOTTED ROAD PRESS

Knotted Road Press fiction specializes in dynamic writing set in mysterious, exotic locations.

Knotted Road Press non-fiction publishes autobiographies, business books, cookbooks, and how-to books with unique voices.

Knotted Road Press creates DRM-free ebooks as well as high-quality print books for readers around the world.

With authors in a variety of genres including literary, poetry, mystery, fantasy, and science fiction, Knotted Road Press has something for everyone.

Knotted Road Press
www.KnottedRoadPress.com

www.ingramcontent.com/pod-product-compliance
Lightning Source LLC
Chambersburg PA
CBHW070034040426
42333CB00040B/1675